The Fundraising Houseparty

HOW TO GET

CHARITABLE DONATIONS

FROM INDIVIDUALS

IN A HOUSEPARTY SETTING

MORRIE WARSHAWSKI,
CONSULTANT

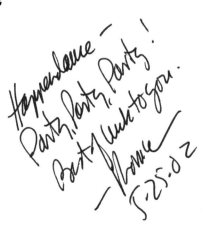

Published by
Morrie Warshawski
1408 W. Washington St.
Ann Arbor, MI 48103
MorrieWar@aol.com
http://www.warshawski.com

ISBN 0-9712789-0-3

Book design by
Murdock Advertising & Design
Ann Arbor, Michigan

The Fundraising Houseparty

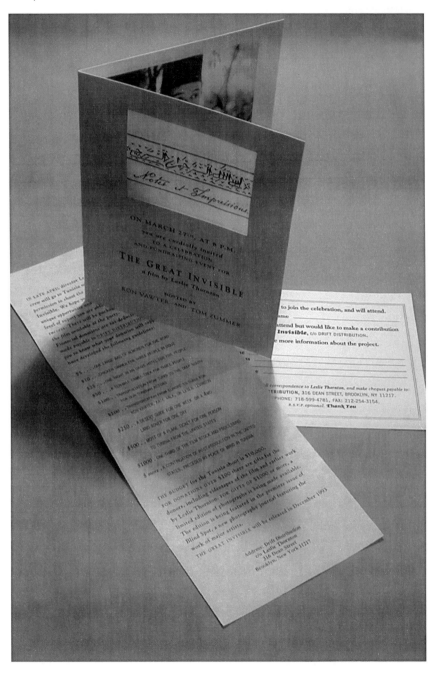

INTRODUCTION

One of the more interesting statistics in the world of fundraising is that individuals account for approximately 87% of all donations for all nonprofit endeavors. Many of my clients assume that the only way to raise support for their projects is by applying for grants—from private foundations, community foundations, government agencies and corporations. Actually, I am a great fan of grants. There is something quite satisfying about creating a lucid and attractive written document that represents you and your organization in a positive light. And, for those of us who are shy people, it's so much easier to drop a manila envelope into a mailbox, than to walk into a room, look someone in the eye and ask them for support. Having said that, it is important to note what all professional fundraisers understand—that the most effective way to get a donation is to ask for it in person.

In my work as a consultant to nonprofit arts organizations and artists—especially independent filmmakers—I have discovered that one pleasant and powerful way to overcome the fear of asking is the fundraising houseparty. The houseparty discussed here is not the kind of fundraising event where people are charged admission, or a premium price for a meal. What I am referring to is the kind of fundraising event that has been popular (with good reason) in political circles for years. The following elements are typical of these events:

Common Elements of a Fundraising Houseparty

- **People receive an invitation to come to a private home.**
- **The invitation makes it clear that the evening will be a fundraising event.**
- **Participants arrive and are served some refreshments.**
- **Participants sit through a brief presentation.**
- **A peer—someone articulate, respected and enthusiastic—stands up and asks everyone present to make a contribution.**

It's just that simple!

This book concentrates on a nuts-and-bolts outline of how to plan for and throw one of these parties. Almost all of the advice has been gleaned from the experiences of individual independent filmmakers, whom I have worked with over the years. I have changed some of the format/content of the instructions I give filmmakers so that the advice will be

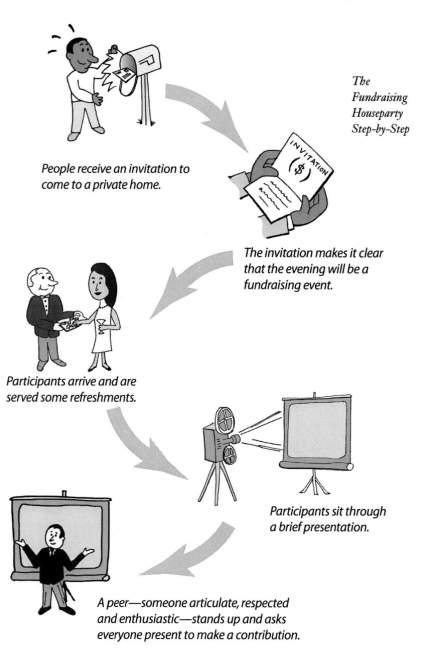

The Fundraising Houseparty Step-by-Step

People receive an invitation to come to a private home.

The invitation makes it clear that the evening will be a fundraising event.

Participants arrive and are served some refreshments.

Participants sit through a brief presentation.

A peer—someone articulate, respected and enthusiastic—stands up and asks everyone present to make a contribution.

germane to almost any type of nonprofit project you might have in mind—a theater's capital campaign, support for your local library, children's play equipment for your community park, etc.

For filmmakers, a typical evening's total usually runs between $3,000 and $7,000. However, I have seen parties bring in far less (a few hundred dollars if you are doing grassroots fundraising with donors of modest means), or far more (tens of thousands of dollars if very wealthy people are invited and pitched properly for the right cause).

Is there a downside to this type of fundraising? Yes—it is labor-intensive, therefore you should make sure that you have a good, hardworking, supportive team making arrangements. This is where a Host Committee can be of great assistance. Also, although these events can be done on a shoestring, it is possible to lose money if you spend too much on refreshments, entertainment, equipment rental or supplies, and printing invitations. Other than that, almost every client I have worked with who threw a fundraising houseparty has been pleased with the results.

In addition to garnering financial donations for your project, these events typically bring you many new friends and supporters. Many people put together a series of parties, sometimes in a number of different cities. This is especially true if your project has different audiences. You might, for instance have a party one night for wealthy

young mothers, and one another night for single young
mothers with more limited resources.

Let me pay homage to the work of Vivian Verdon-Roe and
Peter Adair, two intrepid independent filmmakers who first
introduced me to this idea in the mid-1980s. Additional
thanks go to all the other filmmakers who were brave
enough to try this fundraising tactic, and then share their
successes and failures in order to help others. Also, to Julia
Reichert, a filmmaker who has thrown dozens of parties and
provided very practical advice for this document.

Please feel free to contact me with your own notes about this
"work in progress" so that I can keep passing the information
along to others. And, best of luck to you with your own
houseparty!

Morrie Warshawski
http://www.warshawski.com

KEY ELEMENTS

The prime ingredient to ensuring a successful houseparty is a **Host** who will be willing to open up his or her home and give you access to a mailing list of friends and acquaintances. The ideal host is someone who has already expressed an interest in the project, really believes in what you are trying to do, and has shown a commitment through some kind of donation (money, services or goods).

IT IS CRUCIAL THAT YOUR PARTY TAKES PLACE WHERE THE HOST ACTUALLY LIVES—IN HER HOUSE OR APARTMENT OR LOFT.

Absolutely Critical!

Do not try to throw this event in a restaurant or an art gallery or theater, or any space other than where the host lives. The reason for this is quite simple. There is significance and symbolic power to crossing the portal into someone's private home. The Host is immediately giving a personal imprimatur to you and your project. When she opens the door she is in effect saying to each guest, "Welcome to my home. I believe in this project and want it to succeed so much that I am letting you and many other people invade my private space." When the host is wealthy, you will find that some people will come to the party just because they have always wanted to see the inside of that particular house!

Remember, your host does not have to be wealthy. If you are primarily interested in grassroots fundraising and in building coalitions, then the houseparty can take place in almost any neighborhood and any size of dwelling. At these events, you might be asking for donations in the range of $10 to $100 from each person. When the attendees are middle-income people, you could be looking at suggested pledges in the $25 to $500 range. With wealthy and upper-income people the sky might be the limit.

When appropriate, you could put together a **Host Committee** comprised of a group of people who love you and the project, and who are willing to invite their friends to the soirée. Make sure that the people on the Committee are well respected by your potential donors. When in doubt, take a barometer reading by calling a few people. Another tactic that can add spice to your Committee is to find a local celebrity who will agree to lend her name to the effort. Having a Host Committee on your side can be a powerful way to help ensure good attendance that night, and to pump up interest for your project.

Things you will want to discuss with the Host include:

- **A Good Date and Time for the Event.** Friday from 6 PM to 8 PM is generally an excellent time/day, but anything that will work well for your invited guests and your Host will be fine. Usually, ninety minutes to two hours is plenty of time to allow for the event.

- **The Invitation List.** Make sure that the Host is willing to invite friends and acquaintances. Because so many people are going to RSVP "no," be sure to invite three or four times as many people as you hope will eventually attend. If the host feels nervous about only inviting her friends, then you might add people from your own list as well. But, as much as possible, it's best to have a fairly homogeneous group.

- **The Peer Who Will Make the "Ask."** One of the most important keys to a successful party is your choice of the person who will actually ask people for money that night. The rule is that the person should be a "peer"—someone who is at the same socioeconomic level as others invited to the party, and someone who is well respected by everyone. You and your Host should brainstorm possibilities and come up with just the right person. The ideal peer will be someone who can speak passionately and lucidly about you and your project, and if possible, someone who has already given you support or who

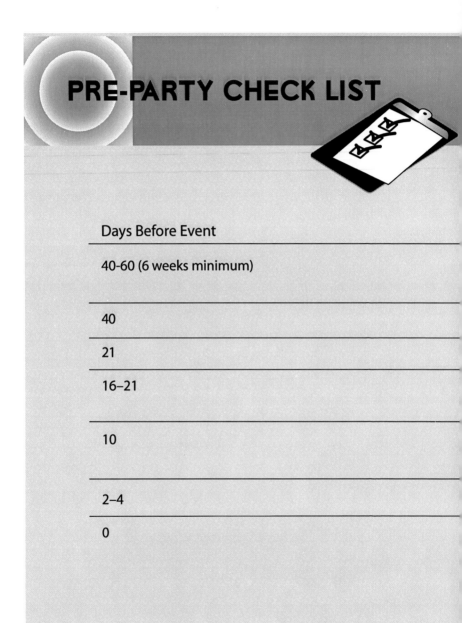

PRE-PARTY CHECK LIST

Days Before Event
40-60 (6 weeks minimum)
40
21
16–21
10
2–4
0

Here is a typical timeline for things to do before the party happens (adapted from Vivienne Verdon-Roe and the Video Project):

Activity

❑ Recruit and have conversation with Host and Co-Hosts.
❑ Set time and date for event. Assign jobs. Agree on program.

❑ Write, design invitation, envelope and inserts and take to printer.

❑ Send invitations with handwritten notes by Host/Co-Hosts.

❑ Call everyone on the guest list for RSVP. Don't skip this step! Calls must come from someone the guest knows.

❑ After contacting all potential guests, check your numbers and deduct around 25% who will probably be "no-shows."

❑ Conduct re-confirmation calls.

❑ Day of the event, plan to arrive at least an hour early to help prepare for the party and check to see that any equipment is working properly.

would be willing to make a donation. Be prepared to help coach the peer on what to say the evening of the party.

- **The Host's Role.** Be sure to let the Host know that her role the evening of the party will simply be to greet people and welcome them. The Host will not be responsible for making the pitch for funds that night. Most Hosts are relieved to hear this! However, if the Host insists on making the pitch then allow her to do so. One thing you should warn the Host is that she is likely to be asked how much she has donated to your project. She should not be shocked when/if this happens. Therefore, it is also important that the Host has already made a donation to your project, or intends to do so publicly the evening of the party.

- **The Invitation.** Decide together what it should look like. You and your team have to be willing to do all the work on the invitation—design, printing, addressing and mailing. However, the Host must permit you to make the invitation look like it is coming directly from her, and she must be willing to write a short note on each invitation, or at least sign each one. If you have a Host Committee, then those individuals will want to sign the invitations going out to their acquaintances. If at all possible, hand address all the envelopes—this is much more effective than using labels. Include an RSVP note that allows people to say they cannot attend but would still like to make a donation, and

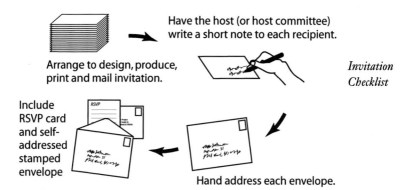

Arrange to design, produce, print and mail invitation.

Have the host (or host committee) write a short note to each recipient.

Invitation Checklist

Include RSVP card and self-addressed stamped envelope

Hand address each envelope.

provide a self-addressed stamped envelope that will go directly to the Host. (Sample invitations are included later in this document.)

- **Follow-up Calls.** If you want to ensure that people attend the houseparty then you, the Host, and/or someone known to the invitees, have to make personal phone calls to everyone invited. Here is what the expert houseparty folks at DC Vote have to say about the subject in their informative on-line House Party Kit (see *Bibliography*):

> *Follow-up calls to confirm that people are in fact coming are absolutely vital. You don't want to hound, but you also want people to realize that this is not a casual party…Two weeks before your house party, start calling everyone on your list…If someone says they cannot attend, then ask them to make a contribution. Make sure you tell them to make their check out to [your organization's*

name] and to send it directly to you. Remember:
Only a small number of people will RSVP without a
call from you…Your follow-up calls will make or
break your house party.

You can supplement personal phone calls with a
series of email reminders (perhaps one per week
beginning four weeks before the houseparty).
Email, however, is no substitute for a personal
conversation.

- **Refreshments.** It is wonderful, and not
  uncommon, for the Host to offer to donate the
  refreshments to be served at the party. However,
  you need to be ready to provide and pay for these
  yourself. The food you serve should be appropriate
  to the setting and to the type of people being
  courted that evening; and the food should be well
  presented as well as non-messy (no red wine or
  cheese fondues). I have attended parties where
  beer and pretzels were served, where fancy tapas
  and Brazilian beer were available, or where finger
  sandwiches accompanied by iced tea were the
  rule. You are not serving a full meal, just enough to
  keep people from being too hungry during your
  presentation later that evening. Again, as with the
  invitations, you and your team must be prepared
  to handle food preparation, service and cleanup if
  the Host does not offer to take care of these.

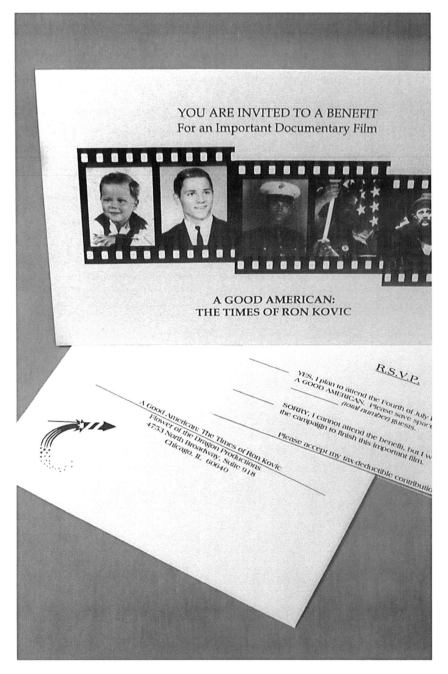

YOU ARE INVITED TO A BENEFIT
For an Important Documentary Film

A GOOD AMERICAN:
THE TIMES OF RON KOVIC

R.S.V.P.

YES, I plan to attend the Fourth of July
A GOOD AMERICAN. Please save space
(total number) guests.

SORRY, I cannot attend the benefit, but I w
the campaign to finish this important film.

Please accept my tax-deductible contributio

A Good American: The Times of Ron Kovic
Flower of the Dragon Productions
4753 North Broadway, Suite 918
Chicago, IL 60640

THE PARTY

The party itself should follow the following rhythm:

- **A period for "Breaking Ice"**
- **Gather guests for a formal sit-down presentation**
- **Host welcomes guests and introduces you**
- **You make a presentation about your project and, if possible, show something from your project (a short video clip, a short theatrical performance, etc.) and field any questions**
- **A peer (someone known and respected by the guests) gets up and asks everyone to make a donation**
- **People are given time to consider the donation**
- **Host and co-hosts thank people as they leave**

PARTY SEQUENCE

*The Party
Step-by-Step*

❑ **Breaking the Ice** *(30 to 45 minutes)*
Provide food and drinks.

❑ **Gather People Together**
Host asks everyone to assemble in specific area.

❑ **Host's Introduction** *(Very brief)*

❑ **Your Presentation** *(7 to 15 minutes)*
*Media presentation followed by
15 to 20 minutes of questions.*

❑ **The Peer Ask** *(Immediately after presentation)*

❑ **People are Given Time to Consider**

❑ **Thank People as They Leave**

Let's look at the party's elements in more detail.

"Breaking Ice"

All you want to do here is allow enough time for people to arrive and get comfortable. Allow thirty to forty-five minutes. This is the time when they will be munching on whatever goodies you've scared up for the evening. Decide if you want to provide alcohol or not. Some people are sensitive about this issue. But if there is no objection to alcohol, don't feel self-conscious about providing it to your guests in moderate amounts. If there is a strong chance that many people will not know one another, then you might provide name tags (with first name in large letters). Have information about your project readily available in a number of locations in the room. You might even provide the host with some visual materials (e.g. photos and posters) to place around the house. Ask the Host and Co-Hosts to circulate around the room and make people feel comfortable. If there is music that is appropriate for your project, you might have that playing in the background. I have even attended events where live music was provided by a salsa band (for a rainforest project), and one where there was an accordion player (for a film to be shot in Russia).

Gathering Guests for Formal Sit-Down Presentation

Prearrange with your Host exactly where in the house you will make the presentation, and make sure you have set up enough comfortable seats for people. Guests will need to be herded into the room and invited to sit down. Remember, people know that they have come to a fundraising party so they are expecting a presentation and a pitch for support. If you are intending to use any equipment, be sure it is set up within everyone's line of vision and that all electrical cords and cables are taped down or placed out of harm's way.

Host Welcomes Guests and Introduces You

This should be the type of very brief "welcome" that makes it clear why the Host has decided to open her house to you and your project. Just a little bit of history about her involvement with you would be appropriate to mention, as well as any heartfelt comments about the project. If the Host is nervous about this, you can help script something for her in advance.

Your Presentation

Luckily, you will not be making the "ask" for funds. That is one of the lovely things about this type of party. However, you are going to have to get up, talk about your project and about yourself and, ideally, show something visual. Be very proactive about what you decide to wear that night. As Julia Reichert says: "Dress as though you look like you could handle money, and dress artistic." The audience will be looking to you for a sense of vision. People will want to know how and why you got involved, how you know there is a need for your project, who it will serve and what you hope it will accomplish, etc. The more emotionally engaging your presentation, the better. This is why a compelling video clip can be a great asset at this party. I recommend a seven-to-fifteen minute clip that looks good (e.g. has no technical problems), and has very strong content —the type that draws viewers in on an emotional level and makes them want to see more. If you are fundraising for something other than a film project, then you might have a slide presentation, or a short theatrical skit using actors from your theater company, or an audio clip. After your presentation, engage in a conversation with the audience and allow people to ask you questions. You might allow as much as fifteen to twenty minutes for this— only as much time as you can maintain a high level of energy. One thing to watch for is a naysayer, or anyone who pulls the group's enthusiasm down with a disparaging comment or question. Have your team, your Host Committee, or a friend ready to jump in when this happens and redirect the conversation if necessary.

The Peer "Ask"

People must be asked to contribute! Do not throw this party without arranging for the peer ask to happen. Do not assume that people are just going to feel good about you and your project and automatically give you a donation. Remember— everyone who has come to this event knows they are going to be asked for money, and their attendance means they are ready and willing to be pitched. The Peer you have chosen will now get up and make a heartfelt plea for support, and directly ask everyone in the room to dig deep into their pockets and give you money. Coach the Peer to be ready to stand up and take over as soon as your presentation is over, or as soon as it becomes obvious that energy has begun to flag. The Peer may talk about how much money is needed, and what different amounts—large and small—will accomplish for the project. The Peer will tell people how they can give—by filling out the pledge cards you've placed on everyone's seats and giving cash, credit card, or checks. The Peer concludes by thanking everyone for coming.

Here is a **Sample Script** you might use for the Peer Ask:

A Sample Script

"First, let me thank you for coming tonight. Everyone here knows me. You know that I don't get up in front of friends very often to make speeches, and you also know that I rarely ask for favors. But, tonight we've just heard about _____, and _____ is something that I care about very deeply. We just have to make sure that _____ becomes a reality. Your donations could make the following things happen: (*list some accomplishments at different donation levels*). I've already given my support through a donation, and volunteering to talk to you tonight. But, _____ 's presentation tonight has moved me once more, and I'm going to give everything I have in my wallet to _____ tonight. Now, I hope each of you will do the same. There's a pledge card on your chair—please fill it out and give whatever you can afford. We'll take a check, cash or credit card tonight, or accept your pledge for a donation you can send in later. If you still have questions about _____ then come up and talk to me in person, or request more information on your pledge card and we promise to get back to you soon. And, thank you again for coming here tonight."

People are Given Time to Consider the Donation

After the Peer ask, provide a number of ways for people to give you their donation. Have baskets available to deposit checks and pledge cards at the entrance to the home, and have volunteers who can walk around the room with small baskets. If you can accept charge cards, you might have a charge machine available at the party. One thing that can help spur people to give, is to arrange before the party for one person who is willing to stand up and publicly commit to making a donation that night. This donor might say something like: "When I came here tonight I was prepared to give $200, but now that I've heard Jane and understand how important this project is, I'm going to write a check for $500 and I urge all of you to do the same, or more." Be prepared to give people additional written information about your project if people request it. If the information is not at the party, then offer to send it the next day. You might also have to provide receipts for people who are giving you cash that night.

Host and Co-Hosts Thank People as They Leave

Allow some time for people to stand up after the presentation and continue eating, drinking and socializing. Shake people's hands and thank them for coming as they leave. Once everyone is ushered out, be prepared to help clean up the house, count your money and celebrate with your Host and Co-Hosts!

The Party's (Not) Over

Most of your work has ended, but there are still a number of very important activities left to accomplish in order to guarantee that your party has been as successful as possible. The first is to be sure to thank your Host and Co-Hosts. A simple note or card should suffice. But if you feel like being a bit more effusive, without spending a lot of money, go right ahead. You might, for instance, send the Host some flowers, or chocolates, or something appropriate to their interests—just so long as it's not too expensive.

You also need to **send "thank you" notes to everyone who came to the party.** For people who made a donation, thank them for the amount they gave you and provide a receipt, if appropriate, for tax purposes. For people who came and who did not contribute, and who also said on their pledge cards, "No, I Do Not Want to Contribute to Your Project at This Time"—also send a note of thanks for taking time out of their busy schedules to attend the party.

For people who came and did not contribute but who said, "I Need More Time to Consider a Contribution"—send a note promising to call soon. **YOU MUST CALL THESE PEOPLE!** A general rule of thumb is that you will bring in an additional 30% of support by making these follow-up calls. The call can be made by you, by someone on your team, by the Host or the Co-Hosts. Generally, you will be responsible for making most of these calls, but it's worth the effort.

There is also one other group of people who need to be contacted—people who said they would come to the party but who did not show up. Call and find out what happened. Give them a description of what they missed at the party, see if they have any questions, and provide them with a chance to make a contribution.

Typical Thank You Cards

Thank You

Your generous tax-deductible charitable donation of $1000 to our project is greatly appreciated. We look forward to presenting the work that you helped make possible soon.

Please find a receipt for your donation enclosed.

Thanks again,

The Project Staff

Thank You

We appreciate the time you spent learning about our project. Please keep the enclosed business card should you decide to make a donation in the future.

Sincerely,

The Project Staff

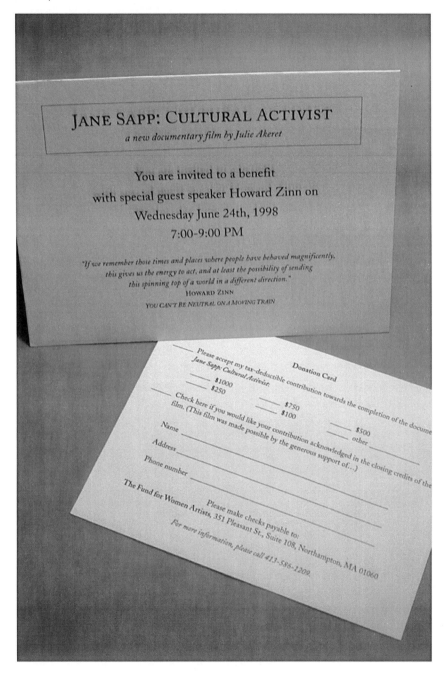

SOME LAST NOTES

Here are some items that deserve a few more comments.

Taxes

I only work with clients who use fundraising houseparties for gaining donations to help create noncommercial projects. In order for you to accept a donation that the donor can claim as a charitable tax deduction, the check must be made out to a nonprofit 501(c)(3) organization. Some people create their own nonprofit organization to accept donations. Many others just use a "fiscal sponsor"—any other legal nonprofit who will agree to accept money on your behalf for the project. The nonprofit could be a media arts center, a hospital, a school, a church—any organization that has 501(c)(3) tax status. The typical arrangement with the fiscal sponsor is that the donor writes the check made out to the fiscal sponsor, noting on the check that it is for your project. The fiscal sponsor then keeps a portion of the check (normally 5% to 10%) and writes a check to you for the difference. Occasionally you might get lucky and find a fiscal sponsor who will perform the service for free. I should note that the kind of party I have described here can and is often used to raise investment monies for commercial projects—but that's another story and beyond the scope of this special report. If you want to pursue investment dollars consult a good investment lawyer!

The Peer Ask

I may not have emphasized enough how important it is to arrange for a peer-to-peer ask. It is a mistake to have the ask made by an expert on the subject, one of your close friends or anyone else who is not a peer of the group. The most effective ask will come when peers ask their own peers for support. Many a party has gone astray because the wrong person made the ask—or in some cases, because no one made an ask!

Video Sample Tape

If asking for funds for a film or video project then you almost have to show something on film or video at this party. I prefer to see a short segment from the piece you are trying to create. A good seven-to-fifteen minute clip that pulls people in and grabs their attention is what I recommend. However, I have had clients show as much as a half-hour and be successful. And I've even seen clips of past work, slide shows, and a taped interview with the filmmakers used to good effect. When in doubt, test the visual material out with a third party. In my experience, the

Holy Grail of sample tapes is one that will make people cry. It is very difficult for donors to say no when they have seen work that moves them emotionally.

Isolation

My very last note is directed to individual artists. One reason I am so fond of this type of fundraising is that it brings an artist out of isolation and into direct contact with potential donors. The fundraising houseparty puts a face on the donation in a non-threatening friendly environment that is far different from other more impersonal fundraising venues such as grants from government agencies and private foundations. And, the houseparty allows the artist to be very proactive with a mechanism that can produce tangible results in a relatively short amount of time.

APPENDIX

SAMPLE FUNDRAISING HOUSEPARTY LETTERS AND INVITATIONS

"A Good American"

Film project by Loretta Smith, includes invitation, RSVP, donor levels

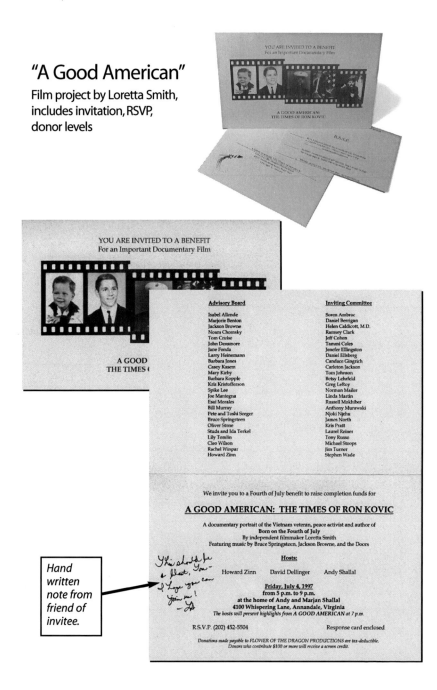

Hand written note from friend of invitee.

A GOOD AMERICAN:
THE TIMES OF RON KOVIC

Donors will be acknowledged in the closing credits of the film
in the following categories:

Saints
Individuals or couples who contribute $10,000 or more.

Angels
Individuals or couples who contribute $5,000 or more.

Benefactors
Individuals or couples who contribute $2,500 or more.

Patrons
Individuals or couples who contribute $1,000 o

Sponsors
Individuals or couples who contribute $500 or

Donors
Individuals or couples who contribute $250 or

Friends of the Film
Individuals or couples who contribute $100 or

R.S.V.P.

_____ YES, I plan to attend the Fourth of July benefit for
A GOOD AMERICAN. Please save space for
_____ (total number) guests.

_____ SORRY, I cannot attend the benefit, but I want to join
the campaign to finish this important film.

Please accept my tax-deductible contribution of:

____ $10,000 ____ $5,000 ____ $1,000 ____ $500

____ $250 ____ $100 ____ Other: $____

NAME _____

ADDRESS _____

_____ ZIP _____

PHONE ( ) _____ FAX ( ) _____ E-MAIL _____

____ My check for the above amount is enclosed.

____ My employer has a matching gift program.

____ You may bill my ____ VISA ____ MasterCard.
(Please indicate which type.)

Number _____ Expiration Date ____

Signature _____

Please make your check payable to
FLOWER OF THE DRAGON PRODUCTIONS and mail it to:

Flower of the Dragon Productions
4753 North Broadway, Suite 918
Chicago, IL 60640
Phone (773) 907-2188   Fax (773) 907-2184

For further information, call (202) 432-3504.

Scale amounts appropriate to your audience.

Put largest amount first.

"Mothers and Daughters: Mirrors that Bind"

Film project by VSM Productions with invitation, RSVP, and film postcard

Mothers and Daughters

MOTHERS AND DAUGHTERS: MIRRORS THAT BIND is a one-hour video documentary that explores the impact of the mother/daughter relationship on a woman's sense of her body, sexuality, and self-esteem. Produced and directed by VICTORIA MILLS, a practicing psychoanalyst, this video aims to challenge stereotypes about the female experience and re-examine the traditional role of motherhood and womens' self-perceptions.

MIRRORS THAT BIND features interviews with women of diverse ethnicities, class backgrounds, and sexual orientations. Using a blend of archival footage, photos, and music, the video asks: how does the mother/daughter relationship affect a woman's individuality and distinctive sense of sexual identity, self-worth, and attitudes? How do race and class impact the mother/daughter relationship? And how are the conscious and unconscious elements of the mother/daughter relationship passed on from generation to generation?

This video will serve as a mirror that reflects back to the audience aspects of themselves and their relationships in a way that opens the door for self-discovery and changes in attitudes and behavior.

MIRRORS THAT BIND is designed for a general TV audience and will be distributed to universities, family planning organizations, junior high and high schools, and women's advocacy groups.

Mirrors that Bind

*This documentary is Fiscally Sponsored by "Women Make Movies."

Film marketing materials serve double-duty as background material in invitation packet.

Words of advice from VSM Productions

Mothers and Daughters: Mirrors That Bind   **Donor Card**

Your contribution will support the editing phase of this documentary. Thank you!

Name_____
Address_____
City_____ State/Zip_____
Ph:_____ Email_____

☐ I am contributing $ _____
☐ I know others who would like to contribute. Please contact me.
☐ I would like to host a fundraiser for the film.

Mirrors that Bind is fiscally sponsored by Women Make Movies. All contributions to the project are tax-deductible. Please make your check payable to Women Make Movies and mail it to: **VSM Productions LLC, 85 Fifth Avenue, Suite 910, New York 10003 Ph: 212-741-3558, Email: vvvjjj@earthlink.com**

You are invited to a

FUNDRAISING PARTY
for
MOTHERS AND DAUGHTERS: MIRRORS THAT BIND
a documentary

Directed by Victoria Mills
Co-Produced by Kathy Leichter
Edited by Flavia Fontes and Shot by Lila Yomtoob

Sunday, May 16th, 1999
4:00-6:00 pm
at the home of Judy Goldring, 465 West End Ave., Apt. 11A
Please R.S.V.P. to (212) 254-6448

Make it clear that it is a work-in-progress—some of our guests thought they would be seeing a finished product.

Prepare for question and answer afterwards. We did this on the fly and were a bit unprepared for some of the things people said.

We thought hard about whether to list specific amounts on the donor card—we decided not to, it worked out fine , but others felt strongly that we should—just something to think about.

We made a questionnaire for people to give us feedback—it was helpful, although not everyone filled them out. Next time we would pass out the introductory letter, support letters, etc. to people personally because not everyone took them even though we put them out all over the room.

We had really good food and flowers and the apartment was gorgeous. That made a difference. The mood was great and fit the film.

"The Great Invisible"

Film project by Leslie Thornton
with hand-worked invitation,
RSVP, and donor level card

With a little bit of manual labor, this vellum window on a textured paper makes a striking, yet inexpensive invitation.

Notes & Impressions.

ON MARCH 27TH, AT 8 P.M.
you are cordially invited
TO A CELEBRATION
AND FUNDRAISING EVENT FOR

THE GREAT INVISIBLE
a film by Leslie Thornton

HOSTED BY
RON VAWTER AND TOM ZUMMER

☐ Yes, I would like to join the celebration, and will attend.

☐ with a guest / Name _____

☐ I am unable to attend but would like to make a contribution to *The Great Invisible*, c/o DRIFT DISTRIBUTION.

☐ Please send me more information about the project.

Name _____
Address _____
_____
Telephone _____

Please address all correspondence to Leslie Thornton, and make cheques payable to:
DRIFT DISTRIBUTION, 316 DEAN STREET, BROOKLYN, NY 11217.
TELEPHONE: 718-599-4781, FAX: 212-254-3154.
R.S.V.P. optional. **Thank You**

IN LATE APRIL director Leslie Thornton and a small crew will go to Tunisia where they have received permission to shoot the final scenes of The Great Invisible. *We hope you can join us to celebrate this unique opportunity and we are deeply grateful for any level of suport you are able to offer towards the trip's success. There will be packages of information about the film available at the party.*
Financial donations are tax-deductible, and should be made payable to <u>DRIFT DISTRIBUTION</u>. *We would like you to know what your donation will support, so we have developed the following guidelines:*

$5 . . . .ONE LARGE BAG OF ALMONDS FOR THE ROAD

$10 . . .CHICKEN DINNER FOR THREE PEOPLE IN DOUZ

$25 . . .ONE NIGHT IN AN OASIS HOTEL FOR FIVE PEOPLE

$50 . . .A TEN-MILE CAMEL TREK FOR THREE PEOPLE

$100 . .TRANSPORTATION FROM TUNIS TO THE DEEP SOUTH FOR OUR TUNISIAN ACTORS

$200 . .TRANSPORTATION FROM EUROPE TO TUNIS FOR RON VAWTER, KATE VALK, OR LESLIE LÉVINSON

$250 . .A DESERT GUIDE FOR ONE WEEK OR A 4WD LAND ROVER FOR ONE DAY

$500 . .MOST OF A PLANE TICKET FOR ONE PERSON TO TUNISIA FROM THE UNITED STATES

$1000 . ONE-THIRD OF THE FILM STOCK AND PROCESSING

$ more .A CONTINUATION OF POST-PRODUCTION IN THE UNITED STATES, PRECEDED BY PEACE OF MIND IN TUNISIA

THE BUDGET for the Tunisia shoot is $10,000. FOR DONATIONS OVER $100 there are gifts for the donors, including videotapes of the film and earlier work by Leslie Thornton. FOR GIFTS OF $1000 or more, a limited edition of photographs is being made available. The edition is being featured in the premiere issue of *Blind Spot*, a new photography journal featuring the work of major artists.
THE GREAT INVISIBLE will be released in December 1993

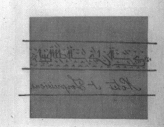

please join us

NADJIB BERBER   TRINH T. MINH-HA
JOHN HANHARDT   ANDREW ROSS
JIM HYDE   SUSAN SLYMOVICS
RON KOLM   KATE VALK

THE GREAT INVISIBLE

is an experimental narrative about Isabelle Eberhardt, the young Russian woman whose life among the desert Arabs of North Africa made her a legendary figure in turn-of-the-century Europe. Disguised as an Arab man, she lived a dual life as both a libertine and an Islamic adept. Reviled by some, worshipped by others, she died in a flash flood in the desert at the age of twenty-seven.

the party will feature

LIVE NORTH AFRICAN MUSIC
ARABIC BUFFET
RECREATION OF A SHEIKH'S TENT
ACTORS AND COSTUMES
and
AN EXCLUSIVE SCREENING OF THE
WORK-IN-PROGRESS

for further information, or to R.S.V.P. (optional), please contact Rachel at (718) 599-4781

"Jane Sapp: Cultural Activist"

Film project by
Julie Akeret with invitation
and donation card

Donation Card

_____ Please accept my tax-deductible contribution towards the completion of the documentary, *Jane Sapp: Cultural Activist*:

_____ $1000   _____ $750   _____ $500
_____ $250   _____ $100   _____ other _____

_____ Check here if you would like your contribution acknowledged in the closing credits of the film. (This film was made possible by the generous support of...)

Name _____

Address _____

Phone number _____

Please make checks payable to:
The Fund for Women Artists, 351 Pleasant St., Suite 108, Northampton, MA 01060

For more information, please call 413-586-1209.

Akeret Films and The Fund For Women Artists invite you to a house party to raise funds for the documentary, *Jane Sapp: Cultural Activist*, Part 2 of *The Activists*, a documentary by independent filmmaker Julie Akeret.

The Activists is a film chronicling the lives and strategies of three little-known but successful social activists. Part 2 will feature the inspirational work of cultural worker and activist Jane Sapp and her group, *Voices of Today*.

Jane Sapp is a powerful song-writer, recording artist, and educator. In 1996 she created *Voices of Today*, an after-school program in Springfield, Massachusetts that uses the arts to encourage "at-risk" teens to express and achieve their dreams.

Historian and Activist Howard Zinn will be the guest speaker, and both Henry Spira (Part 1) and Jane Sapp (Part 2) will attend the event. The evening will also include a screening of footage from Part 1 and Part 2 of the documentary-in-progress.

Wednesday June 24, 1998 from 7:00 to 9:00 PM

at the home of Nisa Zalta and Elan Barnehama

77 Grove Avenue, Leeds, Massachusetts

(Directions on the following page)

Light refreshments and desserts

R.S.V.P 413-586-1209   Response cards enclosed

JANE SAPP: CULTURAL ACTIVIST
a new documentary film by Julie Akeret

You are invited to a benefit

with special guest speaker Howard Zinn on

Wednesday June 24th, 1998

7:00-9:00 PM

"If we remember those times and places where people have behaved magnificently, this gives us the energy to act, and at least the possibility of sending this spinning top of a world in a different direction."
HOWARD ZINN
YOU CAN'T BE NEUTRAL ON A MOVING TRAIN

A Puppet Soirée

A benefit for Jonathan Cross and the Cosmic Bicycle Theatre with coverletter, invitation, and donation levels.

Please join us for

A Puppet Soirée

An evening of intimate puppet performances to benefit
Jonathan Cross and The Cosmic Bicycle Theatre
in their time of need

On Tuesday, February 29th
Leap Day

At the Home of Cheryl Henson
644 Broadway, #7W
(at Bleecker Street)

6 to 9 PM

(Performances scattered around the apartment and throughout the evening)

Suggested donations $25 to $250

RSVP to David Klahr at 212 794 2400 x. 7407

January 25, 2000

Alberta Arthurs

521 5th Avenue
Suite 1801
New York, NY 10175

Dear Alberta,

Jonathan Cross is a very talented artist and puppeteer. His East Village storefront theater, "The Clockworks", which featured the work of The Cosmic Bicycle Theater, was one of the smallest and most charming places to see live puppet theater in the city. Unfortunately, it had to close last fall. We miss his obsessive and unusual sense of humor and hope to see it again very soon.

Jonathan planned to celebrate the 5th Anniversary of his performance space on March 1st, but sadly, they were evicted and can not have their anniversary. To celebrate, I am going to hold a benefit soiree for Jonathan and The Cosmic Bicycle Theater on the previous evening, the evening of February 29th, the only leap year on the Gregorian Calendar ending in "00" since the founding of New York. (1600 was the last "00" leap year, so I am told)

We have invited Jonathan to perform in our next International Festival of Puppet Theater in September 2000. He is going to create a new Dadaist Circus for the mainstage at HERE, but he is living in his storage basement, teaching art and intermittently shopping for unusual antiques for Martha Stuart. Won't you help us to help him?

Please join our benefit committee of presenters, artists, and other friends of puppetry to help make our little soiree a grand event and to show our support for Jonathan, puppetry, and small independent downtown artists. There will be food, wine and miniature puppet performances. We thought we would ask for donations from $25-$250, but he'll appreciate just about anything. It should be a fun evening.

We are making up invitations now, so please expect a call from me or from David Klahr in my office, and please do say that you will join us.

All the very best,

Cheryl Henson

The Committee to Benefit Jonathan Cross and The Cosmic Bicycle Theatre

Leslee Asch	Rob Marx
John Bell & Trudy Cohen	Lynn Moffatt
Elise Bernhardt	Laura Munro
Barbara Busackino	Maggie Robbins
Anne Dennin	Martin P. Robinson
Ed Finn	Mary Rose
Jane Henson	Mark Russell
Heather Henson	Andrew Solomon
David Herskovitz	Richard Termine
Dan Hurlin	Hanne Tierney
Liz Joyce	Basil Twist
Mitchell Kriegman	Laurie Uprichard
Allelu Kurten	David White
Ralph Lee	Jaime Wolf

The Cosmic Bicycle Theatre was evicted from their storefront theater on East 13th Street in the East Village, The Clockworks, late last year. They were scheduled to celebrate their 5th anniversary in their space on March 1, 2000.

The Cosmic Bicycle Theatre was founded in Boston in 1989 by Artistic Director Jonathan Edward Cross. In the intervening 11 years, the company has produced a spectacular array of puppet works, including Moliere's *The Miser, The Marriage of Mother Earth and Father Sky, The Alchemical Work, Dr. Kronopolis and the Time-Keeper Chronicles A Space Opera,* and three miniature works: *Clockwork Universalis (or The Marvels of the Universe); Venus Envy,* and *Thanatopsis.* The company has been featured at P.S. 122, on MTV and its sister network, M2, and at festivals in Europe. They have also appeared several times in the Henson International Festival of Puppet Theater, with another appearance scheduled for September 2000.

$25	Jonathan's Acquaintance
$50	Jonathan's Pal
$75	Jonathan's Buddy
$100	Jonathan's Friend
$125	Jonathan's Dear Friend
$150	Jonathan's Old College Buddy
$175	Jonathan's Cousin
$200	Jonathan's First Cousin
$225	Jonathan's Best Friend
$250	Jonathan's Bestest Friend
$500	Jonathan's Sibling
$750	Jonathan's Life Partner
$1000	Jonathan's Mom
$5000	John Malkovich

Checks can be made out to Jonathan Cross
Donations of $200 or more are tax-deductible if made out to Dance Theater Workshop, designated for the Cosmic Bicycle Theatre

A sense of humor is appropriate and works well for this donation levels card.

34 • THE CHRONICLE OF PHILANTHROPY

"Using Parties to Ease the Process of Asking Friends and Family for Money"

The Chronicle of Philanthropy, February 22, 2001

Using Parties to Ease the Process

Nonprofit board members and donors often have a hard time asking people they know for charitable contributions.

To help ease some of the anxiety associated with raising funds from friends, some nonprofit groups encourage their volunteers to hold parties at their homes as a way to attract donations. At such parties, the organizers usually invite 15 to 50 friends, colleagues, and relatives to enjoy refreshments and hear a short fund-raising pitch.

House parties "take a bit of the pressure off the one-on-one, I'm-asking-my-friend-for-money" approach, says Marla Bobowick, an official at the National Center for Nonprofit Boards, in Washington, who visits trustees nationwide to counsel them about their duties. "We are seeing more organizations say, 'Hey, let's host a dinner in someone's home. We'll bring in some material and it will be kind of casual, but we'll get around eventually to asking for money.'"

Saving a Forest

The Northwest Ecosystem Alliance, an environmental group in Bellingham, Wash., used a series of house parties in 1999 to raise $123,000 for a campaign to save part of a state forest. The group was only given five months to secure the money or the state's Department of Natural Resources would continue to cut down trees.

The urgency of the issue and a fun atmosphere—one party featured a live band—spurred the events' success, says Mary Humphries, the alliance's development director.

Each of the 24 parties started with a 20-minute slide show about the forest, followed by a short fund-raising appeal by the host. If the host was nervous about making a pitch, a charity official offered to set up a practice session beforehand.

After the presentations, a basket with donation envelopes was circulated to help prompt immediate contributions. The charity would sometimes make sure that a small number of loyal donors attended the party—and encourage them to lead the way in writing checks to show what was expected. Then, at the end of each event, charity officials would recruit two participants to hold parties of their own.

"Many people gave much more than they thought they would," says Craig Benton, a recycling consultant who held a party that raised about $18,000. "The checks kept flowing in."

Some lawyers who attended his event asked some tough questions, says Mr. Benton. But charity officials answered them, taking the pressure off him to know every last detail about the campaign.

FUND RAISING   February 22, 2001

# of Asking Friends and Family for Money

"Would I do it again? Yes," says Mr. Benton, who added he felt comfortable making the pitch because he believes in the group's cause. "It was a specific ask for a specific purpose. We could say, Hey, this is what we are going to do with your money."

The charity is planning another round of house parties for a new conservation campaign later this year, with a goal of $250,000.

Wooing New Donors

But money is not always the primary goal of house parties. The International Gay and Lesbian Human Rights Commission, in San Francisco, which fights discrimination, only culls a few thousand dollars from each of its six or so annual house parties. Instead, the group uses the intimate events to woo new donors and strengthen ties with regular contributors.

"It's your opportunity to really meet people face to face and talk to them individually about the work," says Leslie Minot, development director of the commission. "We want people to understand the urgency of our work, but we don't want them to think of us as high-pressure salespeople."

Still, the charity does ask an event's organizer to speak about the group's work and make a plea for donations. "We encourage the host to talk about why they give," says Ms. Minot, "why this matters so much that they are letting 50 people tramp through their homes."
                                        —NICOLE LEWIS

BIBLIOGRAPHY

What follows is a selected list of books and resources to help you with fundraising. For a more extensive listing with hyperlinks visit my website at http://www.warshawski.com.

BOOKS—FUNDRAISING

The Art of Winning Corporate Grants, Howard Hillman. The Vanguard Press.

Catalog of Federal Domestic Assistance. Superintendent of Documents. Washington, DC 20402.

Corporate 500: The Directory of Corporate Philanthropy, Public Management Institute.

Dear Friend: Mastering the Art of Direct Mail Fund Raising, Kay Partney Lautman and Henry Goldstein. The Taft Group, 12300 Twinbrook Pkwy, Suite 450, Rockville, MD 20852.

Designs for Fundraising, Harold Seymour. McGraw.

Directory of International Corporate Giving in America, Katherine E. Jankowski, ed. The Taft Group.

Environmental Grantmaking Foundations 2002, Resources for Global Sustainability.

43 Ways to Finance Your Feature Film, John W. Cones. Southern Illinois University Press.

The Foundation Center: *Source Book Profile: Film, Media & Communications, Comsearch Printouts* (available by subject area on microfiche or in print) *National Guide to Funding in Arts & Culture, Foundation Fundamentals, The Foundation Directory, Guide to Proposal Writing, The Foundation Grants Index Annual* and *Grants to Individuals.* 79 5th Ave., NYC 10003. (800) 424-9836.

Fundraising: Hands-On Tactics for Nonprofit Groups, L. Peter Edels. McGraw Hill.

Fundraising for Social Change, Kim Klein. Chardon Press.

Fundraising on the Internet, Warwick, Allen & Stein, Jossey-Bass.

Grants and Grant Proposals That Have Succeeded,
Virginia White. Plenum, 233 Spring St., NYC 10013.

The Grantseeker's Handbook of Essential Internet Sites,
James DeAngelis, ed. Capitol Publications.

Getting Funded: A Complete Guide to Proposal Writing.
PSU, P.O. Box 1491, Portland, OR 97207.

The Grantmakers Directory (funders of progressive social
change projects). National Network of Grantmakers,
1717 Kettner Blvd, Ste. 105, San Diego, CA 92101.
(619) 231-1348.

*The Grass Roots Fundraising Book: How to Raise Money
in Your Community,* and *Successful Fundraising,*
both by Joan Flanagan. Contemporary Books, Chicago.

*Grassroots Grants: An Activist's Guide to Proposal
Writing,* Andy Robinson. Jossey-Bass.

Guide to California Foundations, Northern California
Grantmakers. (Similar texts are available in many states
including OR, MO, NY, etc.).

How To Write Successful Fudraising Letters,
Mal Warwick. Jossey-Bass.

*Maximum Gifts by Return Mail: An Expert Tells
How to Write Highly Profitable Fund Raising Letters,*
R. Kuniholm. The Taft Group.

Money for Film and Video Artists and *Money for
International Exchange in the Arts,* both from Americans
for the Arts.

Revolution in the Mailbox, Mal Warwick. Jossey-Bass.

*SHAKING THE MONEY TREE: HOW TO GET GRANTS
AND DONATIONS FOR FILM AND VIDEO,* Morrie
Warshawski. Remaining copies currently available only
from the author for $28.95 ($24.95 + $4 pstg) @1408 W.
Washington St., Ann Arbor, MI 48103. E-mail:
MorrieWar@aol.com; or visit his website
www.warshawski.com.

Where the Money Is, and *Where the Information Is,*
H. Bergan. BioGuide Press. Order from
Americans for the Arts, (800) 321-4510 ext. 241.

MISC. PUBLICATIONS

Celebrity Access: How and Where to Write the Rich and Famous, Thomas Burford. Celebrity Access Publications, Mill Valley, CA.

How to Start a Conversation and Make Friends, Don Gaber. Simon and Schuster.

How to Work a Room, Susan Roane. Warner Books.

Not-for-Profit Incorporation Workbook. St. Louis Volunteer Lawyers & Accountants for the Arts, 3540 Washington, St. Louis, MO 63103.

To Be or Not to Be: An Artist's Guide to Not-for-Profit Incorporation, Volunteer Lawyers for the Arts, 1 E. 53rd St., New York, NY 10022.

FUNDRAISING-RELATED WEB SITES

ASSOCIATION OF FUNDRAISING PROFESSIONALS (formerly
The National Society Of Fund Raising Executives)
http://www.nsfre.org

THE CHRONICLE OF PHILANTHROPY
http://www.philanthropy.com

CONTACT CENTER NETWORK, a comprehensive directory
of non-profit organizations and charities:
http://www.contact.org

THE COUNCIL ON FOUNDATIONS
http://www.cof.org

DC VOTE
"House Party Kit"
http://dcvote.org/getinvolved/parties.htm

FOUNDATION CENTER
http://www.fdncenter.org

FOUNDATIONS ON LINE
http://www.foundations.org

GRANTSCAPE
http://www.grantscape.com

MONEY TOUR BY ARTMONEY
http://www.artswire.org/Artswire/www/awtour/
money/page1.html

NATIONAL ASSEMBLY OF STATE ARTS AGENCIES
links to State Arts Councils that have online information:
http://www.nasaa-arts.org

THE NONPROFIT TIMES
A business publication for nonprofit management with a
version available on the web.
http://www.nptimes.com

THE PHILANTHROPY JOURNAL ONLINE
http://www.pnnonline.org

ABOUT THE AUTHOR

 **MORRIE WARSHAWSKI** is a consultant/facilitator/writer who specializes in working in the arts, especially on issues of long range strategic planning. He is the author of a number of books including: A STATE ARTS AGENCY STRATEGIC PLANNING TOOLKIT (National Assembly of State Arts Agencies), and SHAKING THE MONEY TREE: HOW TO GET GRANTS AND DONATIONS FOR FILM AND VIDEO (available only from the author). Warshawski's clients have included: MacArthur Foundation, National Endowment for the Arts, WGBH-TV, Bush Foundation, California Arts Council, American Craft Council, The Council on Foundations and many others. He also has consulted with dozens of independent film/video makers throughout the U.S. You can always find him in cyberspace at: www.warshawski.com.

TO ORDER ADDITIONAL COPIES

Price $14.95 each + $4.00 shipping & handling
for 1st copy ($1.00 s&h for each additional copy)
Send check or money order along
with your name and mailing address to:

Morrie Warshawski
1408 W. Washington St.
Ann Arbor, MI 48103

Please send _____ copies of *The Fundraising Houseparty:*
How to Get Donations from Individuals in a Houseparty Setting
by Morrie Warshawski. Check or Money Order enclosed.

Name: _____

Address: _____

City: _____ **St:** _____ **Zip:** _____

Email: _____